LUCAS
BIRMINGHAM
& BEYOND

LUCAS
BIRMINGHAM
& BEYOND

GORDON BUNCE

JOSEPH LUCAS LIMITED
BIRMINGHAM

Certificate of Apprenticeship

Awarded to ___Robert A. Morris___
of ___101 Deakins Road___
___Birmingham 25___
on completing his ___Machine Tool Fitter___ Apprenticeship
with this Company from the ___10th___ day of
___July___ 1955 to the ___10th___ day of July 1960

Works Training: 15 months Bench, Capstan
& Lathe. 12 months Milling & Shaping,
9 months Grinding & Shaping,
24 months Machine Tool Fitting.

Technical or Commercial College Training
2nd Year Mech. Eng. & 2nd Year City &
Guilds at Garretts Green Technical College.

Certificates gained during Apprenticeship

Joseph Lucas Limited.
_____ Director
_____ Asst. Secretary

The
History
Press

First published in 2004 by
Sutton Publishing Limited

Reprinted in 2017 by
The History Press
The Mill, Brimscombe Port,
Stroud, Gloucestershire, GL5 2QG
www.thehistorypress.co.uk

British Library Cataloguing in Publication Data
A catalogue record for this book is available from the
British Library.

ISBN 978- 0-7509-4033-7

Title page photograph: A certificate of
apprenticeship from Great King Street.

Typeset in 10.5/13.5 Photina.
Typesetting and origination by
Sutton Publishing Limited.
Printed and bound in England.

*This book is dedicated to Jacqueline Hill,
a good friend who by her efforts and research
has helped make this book possible*

Contents

Foreword

by Alton Douglas

'L UCAS MUSEUM REOPENS!' Well, that was my reaction when Gordon Bunce's first book, *Lucas in Birmingham*, was published. Some years prior to that I had enjoyed a visit to the museum in Great King Street. Sadly, the venture disappeared, followed shortly afterwards by the factory itself. Gordon, by collecting memorabilia/ephemera/artefacts (call them what you will), had created a portable pictorial museum. Now you have the opportunity to explore the extension to that mobile Aladdin's cave.

On a personal note, I'm delighted to see Dick Ifield mentioned. I never had the pleasure of meeting him, but in my days as a professional comedian I worked alongside his son, Frank. On a hot summer's day in 1983, he and his mum (Dick's widow, of course) came to our house for tea and to bring me details of one of Dick's inventions for my publication *Coventry at War*. As they drove off, down my narrow drive, Frank managed to take my gatepost with him on the side of his Silver Cloud! As recently as last year I enjoyed ribbing him about it on Ed Doolan's Australian radio programme.

Anyway, this is not about my memories, it's about yours. With this veritable treasure trove in your hands, whether you're a true Lucastrian or, like me, someone who remembers the company with great affection, you're off on a memorable trip into the past. Well done, Gordon!

━━◆━━

Alton Douglas is the author of 38 books.
His biography, The Original Alton Douglas, *was published in 2003.*

Introduction

In 1976 the Chairman of Lucas, Bernard Scott (later Sir Bernard), said 'The idea of publishing a full-scale history of the company has often been suggested, but firmly resisted, the time never being quite right'. The company was still expanding and its pattern not yet fully developed. From a one-man business selling lamps, the company had grown into an international concern with a turnover of £700 million per year, and it was still growing fast. At its height, Lucas employed 80,000 people across 26 main subsidiaries in the UK and 36 more across the world.

Scott went on to praise the success of the company and singled out the major contributors to that success – Sir Bertram Waring, Sir Kenneth Corley and Peter Bennett. 'I think we have cause for pride,' he said, 'and Old Joe, Harry and Oliver [Lucas] would have approved highly of our achievements.'

Some twenty years later the company had closed its doors, having sold off the family silver many times over. But why, and who was to blame for such a successful international company's ultimate failure? Some apportion blame to the management and the chairmen for lack of investment, and others cite union intervention as the cause of Lucas's decline. No doubt we shall never truly know who was to blame for the company's failure, but we should not dwell on the negative. One thing is for sure, Lucas lives on: to this day you can find it everywhere; on the street, at home, all around. The old factories may have a different name over the door, but to many they are still Lucas; former Lucas employees or those connected in some way with the company will retain their happy memories and that is the real purpose of this book – to celebrate and reminisce about the years when Lucas was a great empire.

Sadly it is too late to bring Lucas truly back to life, but that does not mean that we should forget the great days of the company and what it gave people by its very existence. For many, especially through hard times, it gave them a living, for others, myself included, it provided a future – a chance to make something of oneself.

My first book, *Lucas in Birmingham*, dealt mainly with Lucas's Midlands operation. It was received with such enthusiasm that people came forward with many more stories, reminiscences and photographs, and so this second volume has been made possible. I hope that it will prove equally interesting and bring back just as many happy memories of Lucas to the reader.

Gordon Bunce, 2004

Acknowledgements

I would like to offer sincere thanks to the following individuals for their invaluable help in the compilation of this book:

Jacqueline Hill • Eric Collins BEM • Colin Ifield • Bob Lilly • Don Thomas • Paul Oppenheimer MBE • Mary Shears • Val and Malcolm Baldwin • Beryl Jones • Mandy Buckley • Dale Evans • Bill Harley • Marge Summerfield • Jill Chippendale • Nat Gould • David Brown • Sir Kumar Bhattacharyya • Edna Poole • Mary Caldicott • the late John Linforth • Len Bevin • Bob Butler • Evelyn Gill • David Fell • Alf Smith • Rita Bill • Fred Schofield • George Cook • Elizabeth Cornwall • Joy Williams • Jean Robinson • George Butler • Barbara Bullivant • Derek Allen • Bob Dale • Roy Barlow • Barry Brett • Phyllis Peach • Tom Gannon

Special thanks are due to the Gaydon Heritage Museum.

CHAPTER ONE

The Lucas Executive

Perhaps it is unusual to begin the first chapter of a book like this by outlining the responsibilities and duties of the board of directors, but I think it is essential to show that Lucas's board was a very responsible group of people – whatever one may think of the final demise of the business.

The Executive of Joseph Lucas Ltd was responsible to the Lucas Industries Board for the management of the company. The Executive comprised two interdependent bodies: the Policy Executive under the Executive Chairman and the Operations Executive under the Managing Director.

The Policy Executive developed the overall policy and objectives. In addition to the Executive Chairman, its membership included the Managing Director and seven Executive Directors, six of whom were members of the Lucas Industries Board. Each Executive Director had a Group responsibility for one of the following: activities, finance, commerce, technical, policy, strategic planning, manufacturing, engineering and overseas operations. The President of Lucas Industries Inc., USA, was also a member of the Policy Executive.

The Operations Executive was charged with the coordination and implementation of Group policy and objectives as they concerned individual subsidiaries. Under the Managing Director, membership of the Operations Executive comprised the Group Personnel Director and the General Managers of CAV, Lucas Electrical, Lucas Aerospace and Lucas World Service. General Managers of the other major UK subsidiaries and the Group Controller attended most meetings of the Operations Executive.

While the Managing Director provided the formal link between Policy and Operations, the two bodies were essentially complementary in that there was a frequent interchange, with members of each attending the other as necessary.

The Executive was supported by a number of specialist committees which were chaired by the appropriate functional director. Their memberships were drawn both from the central staff and from the operating companies, in order to maintain an interchange between Policy and Operations.

The main committees were:
The Technical Policy Committee
The Manufacturing Policy Committee
The Agreements Committee
The Strategic Planning and Review Team
The Organisation and Executive Planning Committee
The Overseas Capital Provisions Committee
The Insurance Advisory Committee
The Environmental Health and Safety Committee

In addition to the formal committees of the Executive, the Chairman led a special forward-thinking group, concerned with developments in the field of industrial relations.

Joseph Lucas,
1897–1902.

Harry Luc
1902–19.

Lord Bennett,
1937–51.

Sir Bertrar
Waring,
1951–69.

ver Lucas (left) and Peter Bennett contributed
stly different but ultimately successful qualities in
veloping the company between the wars.

low: Oliver Lucas and Peter Bennett were joint
anaging directors between 1923 and 1948. They
e seen here at a long-service presentation, which
s a well-established Lucas tradition.

FINAL MESSAGE FROM SIR BERNARD

In my lifetime with Lucas I have seen its development from what was primarily a Birmingham based and British domestic company into the great international organisation that it is today. I am proud to have been associated with this immense achievement, and I have deeply appreciated the very many generous and complimentary things that people from home and abroad have said and written to me, since the announcement of my retirement, about the part I have played in the enterprise.

I do want to thank very sincerely all those who have sent such kind messages of appreciation and goodwill to me but let me also say this: that any achievement attributed to me has been the result of a combination of my own efforts with those of countless others to whom so much of the credit really belongs.

I suppose from a personal point of view, there is never a right time to end one's tour of duty and I could have wished very much that it had not come to an end when conditions both at home and all over the world seem to be especially difficult.

My experience of being the temporary principal custodian of this great industrial society of ours which is called Lucas has taught me that the first charge of any who hold such responsibilities is to do everything to ensure the continuity of the business; and one of the prime tasks is the provision and preparation of those younger and better qualified men and women to carry on the leadership. Whatever disappointment and setbacks I have suffered, I can number amongst the greatest successes such part as I have been able to play in the development of the new executives and the new managers who will henceforth lead the Company.

As you all know, my place is being taken by Godfrey Messervy with whom I worked first more than twenty years ago when I was General Manager of Lucas CAV and latterly when he has served as Managing Director of Lucas Industries and more recently as Deputy Chairman. I am therefore delighted that the Board has approved his appointment as Chairman, I know that the Company will be in the right hands and that Godfrey Messervy will be supported by a most able and experienced team.

I do not underrate the difficulties ahead; indeed have a sense of some disappointment that I shall not be tackling them with you, for at the root of many of these difficulties lie opportunities for which the technology of Lucas and the personal skills of the people are especially right.

And so, with confidence in these two key aspects, leadership and people, their technical skill and thus their product, I lay down my responsibilities with ease of mind.

Above all, however, when so many are thanking me for what I may have done, I would reply with my own great "Thank You" to Lucas which means the people of Lucas — many of whom I am joining in retirement — for what they have done for me. Thank you.

BERNARD SCOTT

A retirement message from Sir Bernard Scott, Lucas Chairman, 1974–80. This was printed in the Lucas in-house magazine, *Reflections*.

Sir Kenneth
Corley,
1969–73.

Sir Bernard
Scott,
1973–80.

Sir R.G.C.
Messervy,
1980–7.

Anthony Gill,
1987–95.

Jeffrey Wilkinson was joint managing director of Lucas with
Anthony Gill.

J.J. Righton,
Vice-Chairman,
Group Technical Director.

J.H. Williams,
Deputy Chairman
Lucas Aerospace
Holdings.

R.E. March, Group
Personnel Director.

J.W. Bankes,
Group Director,
Strategic Plannin
and Legal Affairs.

A.E. Evetts, Group
Manufacturing Director.

J.W. Shield,
Director and
Treasurer.

C.P.D. Davidson, Group
Commercial Director.

E.B. Wootten,
President of Lucas
Industries Inc.,
USA.

G. Stiley, General
Manager, Lucas World
Service.

These directors of Lucas covered
a period from the late 1960s to
the '80s.

CHAPTER TWO

Noted Sons of Lucas

W ith some 80,000 employees on the payroll, it was to be expected that some individuals would reach greater heights than others. Many 'sons of Lucas' have received major distinctions, so many in fact that it would be impossible to feature them all here.

At Lucas over the years there were many Sirs and many more OBEs and BEMs, and countless further honours. In this chapter I have highlighted some of the most prominent Lucas people who were the recipients of various awards and those who received recognition for contributions not only to Lucas, but also to the motor industry and to the community as a whole.

My first 'noted son' of Lucas is ERIC COLLINS. His background was in toolmaking, and when I first met him in the 1980s he was working in the Lucas Marshall Lake Road toolroom under manager John Butcher. Eric was also convenor of the Amalgamated Engineering Union (AEU) at Marshall Lake Road, and it was in this guise that I came to know him better. I had been appointed factory manager and in my dealings with him as a union representative I found him to be very much removed from what one would expect a shop steward to be like. Rather than table-thumping and raised voices, Eric always strove to resolve situations calmly. He was razor-sharp and very direct in his approach.

Eric always had a special interest in politics, and between 1963 and 1969 he served on Birmingham City Council, and later on Meriden Council. He was appointed Mayor of Solihull in 1979, a role in which he was ably supported by his wife, Winifred. Perhaps his greatest achievement was receiving the BEM from Lord Aylesford, Lord Lieutenant of Warwickshire and Queen's Representative. The award was made at Packwood House and was undoubtedly a very proud day for Eric and his family.

He carried on representing his council ward of Chelmsley Wood, Solihull, well into the 1990s. Today Eric is retired, though he is still sought-after to impart his advice on many matters. He is without a doubt a very worthy son of Lucas.

Eric and Winifred Collins, Mayor and Mayoress of Solihull, 1979.

uncillor Eric Collins, Mayor of Solihull, is presented with eleven new gold and silver links for the Solihull ain of office by Jeffrey Wilkinson, Divisional Managing Director of Lucas Industries, and Ronald Marsh, oup Personnel Director.

c and Winifred Collins greet Prime Minister Margaret Thatcher on her visit to Solihull, 1979. Also in the otograph are Lord Thornycroft, Chairman of the Conservative party, and singer Petula Clark.

Eric Collins lands an impressive left hook on boxer Henry Cooper.

Ron Flint introduc
HRH the Duke of
Kent to Eric Collin
during a visit to th
Marshall Lake Ro
factory in 1980.
Lucas Chairman
Godfrey Messervy
looks on.

Ke Hua, the Chinese Ambassador, and his wife are
·eted by Eric and Winifred Collins, who escorted them
nd the Lucas factory at Marshall Lake Road as part of
official visit in 1979.

c Collins in his mayoral robes, 1979.

Eric Collins shakes hands with Lord Aylesford, Lord Lieutenant of Warwickshire, on the occasion of receipt of the BEM, early 1980s. A shown are David Barrows, Technic Director, Ken Wills, General Mana of Lucas Electrical, Winifred Collin and Douglas Waltham, Director of Engineering.

Eric and Winifred with their guests at Packwood House. Among those in the group are Sheila Barlow, Fred Schofield, Gordon Bunce and David Barrows.

Eric Collins celebrates his appointment as mayor with some leading Solihull councillors, 1979.

RICHARD 'DICK' IFIELD was without doubt a prolific inventor, yet in the 1930s few, if any, knew of him or his work. Though his ancestors hailed from the town of Ifield in Sussex, Dick was an Australian born and bred. Life in the southern hemisphere had been quite lean for Dick and his family, so in 1935 they came to England. Dick found work with the Bendix Brake Company, which was owned by Lucas. Bendix was an ailing company and struggled to gain a reasonable foothold in the market, so Lucas appointed Captain Irving as General Manager and Chief Engineer to see if he could restore its fortunes. Bendix's major competitor at the time was Girling, which had a much better reputation in the brakes market. Lucas, as Bendix's parent company, took the brave decision to buy Girling out. Dick's contract, however, was with Bendix, and this must have been a cause for concern to him. His contract was for £100 per invention, beginning with his differential designs. This was a huge amount of money at the time, and had allowed him and his family to move into a large house near Solihull. It also funded the purchase of a car – a Rover. Dick was now moving up in status, and he was provided with a company car, this time a Riley Kestrel (which incidentally, featured one of his own differential designs).

Dick Ifield.

Some prominent Lucas personalities involved in gas turbine development during Dick Ifield's time. Left to right: Dr John Clarke, Joe Righton, John Morley

Below: Some of the gas turbine team at a farewell dinner on the occasion of Dick Ifield leaving for Australia.

His differentials were becoming better known and acclaimed, but the old Bendix company had reluctantly cancelled their contract with him, and once again he found himself without a sponsor. His friend and colleague Captain Irving tried his best to help by introducing Dick to the movers and shakers on the automotive engineering circuit: first to the chief of Alvis, Captain Black, and later to Rolls-Royce. Eventually Dick received a telephone call to say that Dr Watson from Lucas (the Group Chief Engineer) wanted to meet him and see his work on helical gear pumps. Sadly this particular invention did not meet with Lucas's approval, but it did allow Ifield to get a foot in the door. He was invited to submit more work to Watson, much of which was to lead to acceptance.

LUCAS

Presented
by the Directors to

Richard Joseph Ifield

as a mark of appreciation &
goodwill upon completing

Twenty-Five Years
Loyal and Efficient Service
with

Joseph Lucas Ltd.
AND
ASSOCIATED COMPANIES

1965

A long-service certificate presented to Dick Ifield on completing twenty-five years of loyal service.

The Ifield boys in Australia, 1949.

At one point Lucas found itself with a problem: its pumps were failing when tested with kerosene on load tests. This was a very gruelling pump test, and all the pumps which were submitted failed, except Ifield's. This success led to Dick gaining direct praise from both Oliver Lucas and Dr Watson, who were keen to keep him and his inventing skills as an important part of the Lucas company. Dick was offered a new contract featuring a £230 retaining fee, a cash sum of £1,000, a salary of a further £1,000 per year and a £400 annual bonus. Dick was heard to say 'I have never felt so rich!' Life had completely turned around for Dick and his family since the tough early years in Australia. Ever the careful man, he decided to buy his company car . . . and kept it for a further 10 years. It is still in his family to this day – his son having acquired it.

Many people commented to Dick over the years that with all the inventions he had to his name, he ought to have been a millionaire. Despite his shrewdness with money, it was never so important to him as recognition for his work. He was a prolific and successful inventor, and a great deal of his work was associated with the aero gas turbine engine. He had his own office at the Shaftmoor Lane factory and a staff of four, and dealt with many major companies including Rover, Rolls-Royce, Metropolitan Vickers, Armstrong Siddeley, de Havilland, Bristol and Napier, to name but a few.

In 1940 Dick took the decision to move to London, taking up office at the CAV site in Acton. He reasoned that living in the capital could not be any more dangerous than living in Birmingham – a point he may have reconsidered when the Nazis began to use V2 flying rockets as part of their blitz on London in the autumn of 1944. The Ifields rented a house overlooking Park Royal and it was here that their fifth son, Geoffrey, was born. CAV had lost a great deal of its design and production knowledge when their partner company, Bosch, recalled all their engineers to Germany at the start of the Second World War. Dick found himself less than welcome at CAV and found he had no alternative but to relocate himself and his small team back to Shaftmoor Lane, Hall Green.

gathering of the Ifield family in 1959. Among those present are Dick, Jim, Colin, Muriel, Bob, John, Jan, nk and David.

By 1947 Dick was becoming homesick and thoughts of a return to Australia were beginning to cross his mind. It had been over twelve years since he and his wife had seen their parents. The couple also thought it would be more beneficial for their sons to grow up in Australia. Dick informed a special committee of executive directors of his decision and the family moved back to Australia in 1948. He bought a property in Dural which became the first headquarters of the family business R.J. Ifield & Sons Pty Ltd, but the family were soon on the move again, this time to a sprawling property with 89 acres, well-suited to a family of boys.

When settled back in Australia, Dick was appointed Special Duties Director to the Gas Turbine Company (which was later to become Lucas Aerospace. His remit was to attend board meetings on behalf of Lucas around the world. Things gradually began to change. New faces were appearing in the company, but Ifield still remained part of the Lucas scene – it seemed that his reputation held a great deal of importance for many major Lucas customers, Rolls-Royce included, which continually enquired if he was still a part of the organisation. Dick finally resigned from Lucas in 1970 and took up an executive role in the family business.

Sadly Dick Ifield died in the 1980s, but some of his sons carry on the family firm. Another of his sons, Frank Ifield, became a successful and well-known recording artist with a special talent for yodelling. He is still popular today and spends much time performing in the UK.

Dick with his sons at a family gathering, possibly Frank's weddir

Singing star Frank Ifield.

GODFREY MESSERVY was born in Derby into a family involved in the motor industry. When the Second World War broke out he was still a teenager, but in 1943 he enlisted in the Royal Engineers and in the years that followed he gained a commission. He joined the 1st Parachute Squadron of the Royal Engineers and after seeing active service in Norway he transferred to the 5th Airborne Divison and served two years in Palestine, by which time he had achieved the rank of captain.

In 1949 he joined Lucas CAV at grass roots level as a production trainee and was swiftly promoted to foreman in 1951. Within three years he was a superintendent. Further promotions came his way and after a stint as Chief Quality Engineer he became a director of CAV in 1963. Still climbing the career ladder, Messervy was invited to join the Executive Board of Joseph Lucas, was appointed Managing Director in 1974, Deputy Chairman in 1979 and finally Chairman in 1980.

Godfrey Messervy
before receiving his
knighthood.

During Messervy's tenure as Chairman he never shirked from challenges and was always determined to stick to his principles. In the 1980s he was quoted as saying 'Lucas will measure up to the demands that the British-based motor industry will impose . . .'. He was acutely aware of the fact that he was taking the reins of a company at a critical period. As Chairman his first commitment was to maintain the company's rate of development, which was costing around £40 million per year. He strove to gain Lucas an even higher percentage of the market share through its vast experience and technological know-how, and enabled it to penetrate the overseas market very successfully. Sadly though, not even Godfrey Messervy's determination could halt the eventual decline of Lucas, which began in the 1980s.

A married man with two daughters and a son, Godfrey was a council member of the Birmingham Chamber of Industry & Commerce and a Liveryman of the Worshipful Company of Ironmongers. Away from his taxing role at Lucas he found relaxation in a number of hobbies, ranging from motorcycling and motorsport to farming, photography and aviation. Godfrey Messervy was knighted in 1986 and retired from Lucas in 1987. He was very much admired and respected and was an extremely worthy Chairman. He died on 12 October 1995.

Godfrey Messervy (third from left) with Lucas employees who received the Chairman's Awards in 1985 Suggestion Scheme. The top award went to Peter Weller, an electrical maintenance engineer from Lucas CAV at Rochester, who received £2,500 for devising a portable setting aid for Hartridge product test machines.

nk Morris is presented with an
ard for twenty-five years' service by
lfrey Messervy.

Don Thomas receives a watch from
Godfrey Messervy to commemorate
twenty-five years' service with Lucas.

lfrey Messervy makes a
sentation to a CAV employee. This
tograph was taken when he was
eral Manager of CAV during the
70s.

PAUL OPPENHEIMER graduated from London University in 1954 with a first-class honours degree in Mechanical Engineering. He subsequently obtained a Masters in Thermodynamics from Birmingham University a year later, qualified as a Chartered Engineer and was elected as a Fellow of the Institute of Mechanical Engineers.

After completing a five-year engineering apprenticeship at BSA Tools at Marston Green, Birmingham, Paul worked in other parts of the BSA group and participated in the development of the first British automotive turbochargers for diesel engines, using his knowledge of thermodynamics to design the compressor and turbine.

Oppenheimer joined the Lucas organisation in August 1958 as a Nuclear Project Engineer in the Lucas Group Research Centre, The Radleys, Kitts Green, Birmingham, working for Dr Bill Arroll, the Director of Research. This role offered opportunities within the developing nuclear engineering industry in the UK, but despite several interesting efforts to utilise specific Lucas capabilities within a nuclear environment, this attempt at product diversification did not succeed.

Paul Oppenheimer MBE.

...c Halliwell, Paul Oppenheimer and Ken Barling at a Girling reunion.

In January 1962 Paul was transferred to Lucas Girling at Tyseley, where he carried out various engineering liaison duties in Europe and overseas. Working as a Project Engineer for the Engineering Director, Arthur Goddard, Paul assisted with the introduction of disc brakes in production cars at Fiat and Alfa Romeo via the Lucas office in Milan. After mastering the braking system performance calculations (data sheets), he joined the Overseas Operations Department under Vernon Hawker and Graham Lock, selling and licensing Girling products, notably disc brakes. Japan became Paul's principal territory, and, after numerous visits, Paul lived in Japan for nearly a year to provide the technical liaison for the growing number of important Girling licences in Japan.

In 1970 Paul inherited the Girling regulations duties. He soon joined the Society of Motor Manufacturers & Traders (SMMT) Brakes Committee in London, meeting fellow specialists from major motor manufacturers. As a delegate from the SMMT, Paul represented the UK motor industry at international committee meetings of the European vehicle and components manufacturers' associations in Paris and at corresponding government committee meetings of the EEC in Brussels and the United Nations Economic Commission for Europe in Geneva. These organisations developed uniform vehicle regulations for the international 'type approval' of road vehicles, systems and components. Paul made a special study of the road vehicle braking regulations in Europe and he became an influential member of all the national and international industry and government committees. He has analysed the corresponding US Federal Braking Standards and he initiated the harmonisation of the European and American standards. His Lucas Girling 'Yellow Book', incorporating the official texts of the various braking regulations, became an immediate bestseller within the worldwide motor industry.

Paul has become the guru of braking regulations and has made many technical illustrated presentation on this subject, notably at the Society of Automotive Engineers (SAE) Congress in Detroit, gaining the SAE's Distinguished Speaker Award and the SAE Award for Excellence in Oral Presentation.

Paul completed twenty-five years' service with Lucas in 1983 and received his carriage clock at a ceremony at Great King Street. In October 1988 the Lucas Girling site at Tyseley was closed and Paul was moved to the Lucas Automotive Advanced Engineering Centre in Shirley.

Paul receiving the European Commercial Vehicle Safety Award from Professor Von Glasner of Daiml Chrysler in Munich, 2001.

...cas car braking
...mposium held at Stratford-
...on-Avon, 1993. Paul is
...rd from the right on the
...ck row.

...ul with copies of his book,
...m *Belsen to Buckingham*
...*ace.*

Jack Lowerthal, Roy Garner, Wendy Marsh and Ken Barling at the 1994 Girling reunion that P Oppenheimer organised.

Many of his papers have been published by the Institute of Mechanical Engineering in the UK and by the SAE in America and Paul has been awarded several prestigious prizes. In 1990 Oppenheimer's unique expertise was recognised in the New Year's Honours List with the award of an MBE for services to the British motor industry, and in 2001 he received the European Commercial Vehicle Safety Award.

After thirty-two years with Lucas, Paul officially retired in August 1990, but he continued to maintain his interest in braking regulations as an independent consultant until December 1996. In 1994 Paul organised a Girling Tyseley reunion which attracted more than 100 colleagues, and since then five further reunions have confirmed the camaraderie and happy days at Tyseley.

In September 1996 Beth Shalom of the Holocaust Centre near Nottingham, published Paul's book *From Belsen to Buckingham Palace*. This was a surprise to Paul's colleagues at Lucas, who were totally unaware of his wartime experiences as a Holocaust survivor. Nowadays Paul presents his eyewitness account of the Holocaust to students in schools to prevent prejudice, discrimination, racism, persecution and genocide.

Paul has been married to Corinne for forty years, they live in Solihull, and they are blessed with three children and five grandchildren.

CHAPTER THREE
Royal Visit

On 3 November 1955 the young Queen Elizabeth and her husband the Duke of Edinburgh made an official visit to Lucas Great King Street, Birmingham. It was not a particularly warm day, but it stayed dry for the thousands who lined the streets to catch a glimpse of the royal party. As the hour of the Queen's arrival approached the people lined up against the barriers outside were getting excited, and the atmosphere inside the factory was electric. The employees of this giant firm had spent days getting the factory looking in pristine condition for her visit. With so much bunting festooned around the walls and gangways, the plant looked more like Santa's grotto than an engineering works! Not since the coronation of King George VI in 1937 had the Great King Street site been so lavishly decorated.

A great hush fell outside the factory and then a mighty roar went up as the royal cars came into view. There was a great deal of cheering and flag-waving as the Queen's car arrived at the entrance. The Chairman of Lucas, Bertram Waring, was waiting on the steps of the Personnel Block, along with the Lady Mayor of Birmingham and other civic dignitaries to greet the Queen and Prince Philip. The Queen acknowledged the crowd with a wave and another great cheer went up.

The welcome speech from the Chairman was delivered and the royal party entered the building with a final wave from the Queen. Light refreshments were on hand for the party and then the tour of the factory began. The party walked amid the rows and rows of machines, stopping here and there for a chat with the operators, who had been instructed to remain at their machines, and not to flood the gangways to get closer to the royals. It must have been a great honour for those who were lucky enough to get to talk to the Queen. Sadly, royal visits do not last very long, and it was soon time for the party to leave for their next engagement. The workers inside all crowded to the windows for a final glimpse of the Queen and Prince Philip before their departure.

It had been a glorious day for everyone concerned and would not be forgotten in a hurry.

The directors' entrance dressed for the Queen's visit with royal blue and gold crowns.

e royal party arrives and Sir Bertram Waring greets the Queen.

e party is led up Little King Street between the two factories.

Her Majesty the Queen with Lord Peter Bennett (left) and Sir Bertram Waring (right). The rest of the pa
follows on behind.

colourful display
the factory floor
the royal tour.

The Queen is introduced to the General Factory
Manager, L.C. Leech.

Employees' families take the tour of the factory after the Queen's departure.

CHAPTER FOUR

Lucas Before 1945

Lucas was well known for its enlightened attitude to employees' welfare, and much was done by the company both materially and financially to promote their interests. One organisation that the company supported was the Supervisors' Association, which initially promoted good will at supervisory level; such was its success, though, that it later attracted many other staff – not just supervisors – and from all factories.

Each factory had a branch of the association, and each year an election was held to elect a chairman, treasurer and, most importantly, an activity organiser. Dances, parties, outings and sports visits to other factories were all arranged – all heavily subsidised by the company. During the 1980s, as Lucas found itself in financial difficulties, cutbacks took their toll on all these social events. Children's and pensioners' parties had to end, and sports fields were sold off for housing. Most of Lucas's welfare activities finished at this time, in the opinion of many severing the close link between employer and employee.

bremen's outing in October 1932.

THE FUNERAL OF MR. JOSEPH LUCAS

An Old Interesting Newspaper Cutting

A CUTTING from the "Birmingham Post" of January, 1903, which describes the funeral of the Founder of the Firm has been sent to Mr. Oliver Lucas, and as we thought all our readers would be very interested to read it we print it below :—

The funeral of the late Mr. Joseph Lucas, a well-known figure in the temperance life of Birmingham, and who died at Naples on December 27th, took place yesterday in the churchyard at Moseley. At one o'clock an impressive funeral service took place in the Temperance Hall, Temple Street, and was largely attended by the friends of the deceased gentleman and by the general public. The coffin, which was covered with a number of beautiful wreaths, occupied a position underneath the platform rails, and was flanked by a profusion of palms. The service was conducted by the Rev. C. E. Beeby, Vicar of Yardley Wood, assisted by the Rev. R. Gray, Baptist, and the Rev. J. Loosmore, Congregational; and it commenced with Chopin's "Funeral March," played on the organ by Mr. Ernest A. Thompson. The Rev. C. E. Beeby then pronounced the first portion of the service, which was followed by a reading of the Scripture : "Lord, Thou hast been our refuge." Then came the singing of Longfellow's "Psalm of Life" to Haydn's swelling music. After the reading of the second portion of Scripture, "Now is Christ risen from the dead," Miss Nellie Pritchard sang "O rest in the Lord," with exquisite tenderness. The hymn, "He liveth long who liveth best" was then sung, followed by prayer offered by the Rev. C. E. Beeby, and the whole congregation joined in the rustling whisper of the Lord's Prayer. The Birmingham Temperance Philharmonic Choir then sang "No shadows yonder" (Gaul). Then came the final prayers, and the audience stood reverently as, to the strains of Handel's Dead March in "Saul," the coffin was borne from the hall by a company of the deceased's workmen. The funeral cortege afterwards proceeded to the churchyard at Moseley, where the committal service was conducted by the Rev. C. E. Beeby.

Then follows a very long list of the mourners, individuals and societies.

The mourners were : Messrs. H. Lucas, C. Lucas, B. Lucas, J. Bamford, W. J. Perkins, G. Thomas, H. Porter, sen., H. Porter, jun., W. Lucas, E. H. Lucas, F. Lucas, T. Randall, T. E. Bench, G. Owen, A. T. Powell, B. Steeley, B. Owen, H. Owen, C. Bamford, J. R. Atkins, H. Johnson, C. Hall, C. Y. Hopkins, J. Shilton, the Rev. R. Gray, the Rev. C. E. Beeby, the Rev. J. Loosmore, Messrs. Thompson, Goodall, Pierce, Green, Broadbent, Bartleet, Norfolk, Galloway, Davy, Griffin, Vickery, Richards, Perry, sen., Jackson, Wankling, Jenkins, Evans, Edwards, Ansell, Danks, Parks and Eggington.

The following deputations were present :—Birmingham Temperance Society and Temperance Hall Company, Messrs. J. Archer, H. Bowley, R. Breakspear, R. C. Griffin, G. W. Keesey, J. Macmillan, J. Manning, F. Mills, S. E. Short, T. Hewins, W. Wilde, E. L. Tyndall, J. Derrington, J. H. Lear, Caton, S. Goodyear, and Miss L. B. Ward; stewards of the society, Mrs. Binns and Mr. T. Gravey; Temperance and Philharmonic Choir, Messrs. E. A. Thompson, A. S. Fowles, Holt, and Lawman; United Kingdom Alliance Messrs. J. Moseley, J. Pearc Derrington, D. Arkinstall, W. Priest man and W. J. Holmes; Birmingham and Midland Band of Hop Union, Messrs. A. E. Butler, Lapwood, J. Lawson, and Councillo A. J. Herrick; the Police Institute Mr. and Mrs. J. T. Wilson; Unite Kingdom Band of Hope Union, M W. T. Stanton; North Birmingham and District Band of Hope Unio Messrs. A. Wiseman and T. Nicklin Midland Temperance League, M T. Ainsworth; Sunday Closing Asso ciation, Messrs. J. Roles and Moore; Temperance Ironside Messrs. Griffiths and Ekins; Bir mingham City Mission, Mr. A. B Barker; Church of the Saviour, M C. L. Nott; St. George's Ward Poo Christmas Fund, Mr. Henry Court ney; Salvation Army, Mr. W. H Dunkley; Independent Order o Good Templars (Warwickshire an Worcestershire), Independent Orde of Rechabites, Messrs. W. Page an Beck, J. Wagstaff, D.C.R., an Harris; Gospel Temperance Mission Messrs. F. H. Butler and J. Living stone; Tamworth Band of Hop Union, Messrs. Allton and Hampton National Commercial Temperanc League, Messrs. J. Hood, G. Well and G. Meredith. There were als representatives of the Middlemor Homes and the Institution for th Blind. Among the wreaths wer those sent by Mrs. Lucas and M Bernard Lucas, Mr. and Mrs. Harr Lucas, Mr. and Mrs. Chris. Luca Mr. and Mrs. Perkins, Mr. an Mrs. Bamford, Mr. and Mrs Thomas and family, the employee the members of the office and staf Superintendent Tozer (of the Bir mingham Fire Brigade), and the Bir mingham Temperance Society.

This report of Joseph Lucas's funeral was first published in the *Birmingham Post* in January 1903, and la reported in *Reflections*.

...ve: A group of Lucas ...ckmen in the early ...entieth century. ...the top of the ...otograph can be ...n part of a Lucas ...vertising poster ...ring the famous 'King ...he Road' slogan.

...ployees from Lucas ...at King Street on an ...ing in the 1920s.

Lucas football team, winners of the Dewar Trophy Shield 1921/22. Third from the left on the middle row John (Jack) Gibbons, who was a polisher at Great King Street.

A Lucas Service advertisem on a van, c. 1929.

TO "THE GOVERNOR"

IF you were to enter "the Governor's" office in Great King Street, you would be greeted by a very hearty old gentleman who refuses to grow old and, although he is now in his 81st year, still assists to guide the progress of the business.

Mr. Harry Lucas was born on the 10th February, 1855, and was about 18 years of age when his father, the late Mr. Joseph Lucas, laid the foundations of the *House of Lucas*. From the very first, he was his father's right-hand man, and to him is due the steady and continuous growth of the business up to the outbreak of the Great War. After the death of his father, in 1902, he became Chairman, as well as Managing Director of the Company, which offices he held until increasing deafness made it practically impossible for him to carry on these onerous duties.

Always keenly interested in the manufacturing side of the business, Mr. Harry Lucas was in the habit of trying out for himself any new production, and he had to be personally satisfied regarding its suitability—and reliability—before he allowed it to be placed on the market. In the early days, for instance, he tested cycle lamps himself, under practical road conditions. A lamp would be fitted to a bicycle which Mr. Harry rode to prove whether the lamp would remain alight and stand up mechanically to really rough going. With the dawn of the motoring era, Mr. Harry had one of the first ten cars in Birmingham, and soon commenced the production of oil lamps and accessories for automobiles.

Over 22 years ago he started what was probably the first Works' Savings Bank in Birmingham. Some thousands of employees now have accounts with the *Lucas* Savings Bank and the number is steadily increasing. Mr. Harry Lucas is very interested in philanthropic work and was one of the founders of the Birmingham Rowton House, whose chairman he has been for many years. Mr. Lucas, who is to-day Consulting Director, is keenly interested in the activities of the *Lucas* Sports Club, and both Mrs. Harry Lucas and himself have been frequent visitors at the various social functions. He never misses a Sports Day despite other business. "No," he was once heard to say, "I am going to see my people enjoy themselves."

Like his father, Mr. Harry Lucas has very definite views on some matters and the courage to express them. He has always shown keen discernment of character which was never better illustrated than when selecting workpeople. Everyone knew then as they know now that it is no use bluffing "the Governor." His interests are varied, including literature and works of art, and he is also a student in Egyptology. He has an uncommonly interesting collection of books, including some rare and beautiful examples of printing and book-binding. His collection of pictures is one of the best private collections in the City of Birmingham. He has given pictures and other works of art to the Birmingham Art Gallery, and has long been interested in the Birmingham Society of Artists and has made provision for annual awards in the Arts and Crafts section.

Mr. Harry Lucas is also well-known as a *raconteur*. He has a fund of good stories and anecdotes on which he has often drawn to enliven meetings. Here is an instance of Mr. Harry's dry humour: A cyclist had returned an old lamp which he said he had had in constant use for twenty-two years, during the whole of which time he had never had a moment's trouble with it or spent a penny in repairs. The cyclist suggested that we might like to take and keep the old lamp as an example of good service, and give him a new one free of charge. "Ah!" said Mr. Harry, "it's a pity it didn't last him a few more years—then we might have given him a new bicycle as well."

At a Work's meeting, at which Mr. Harry presided, a foreman made a statement that in order to carry out successfully some experimental work which was in hand, certain things would be necessary. This was challenged by others present, and finally Mr. Harry said that the idea would be tried for a week and if it was satisfactory then he would buy the person who suggested it a new hat. At the end of the week Mr. Harry went to the Foreman's Office and calmly dropping a golden sovereign on the desk said: "There you are, buy yourself a new hat."

Here is an example of his sturdy determination. A little while ago there was a Works' Outing, with British Camp in the Malvern Hills as its venue. The party travelled by car as far as they could and then had to climb the remainder of the distance; anyone who knows this part of the country will realise what a steep climb it is. When he alighted from his car, someone offered Mr. Harry an arm, but it was courteously declined with the words: "No, thank you, I prefer to go up under my own power."

On February 10th, Mr. Harry Lucas celebrated his 80th birthday, and on behalf of all Members of the Staff of JOSEPH LUCAS LIMITED and its Associated Companies we cordially congratulate "the Governor" and we hope that he will be spared for many more years.

s article appeared in *Reflections* in 1939.

Workers leav
Lucas Little
King Street o
a Birmingha
Corporation
1935.

The Lucas works band looking very dapper, 1935.

Harry Lucas.

'The Governor', Harry Lucas, seen here in 1884 with his penny farthing. Always a keen cyclist, he was a member of Birmingham Tricycle Club.

A proposed solution to expected parking difficulties in New Street, Birmingham, based on one in New York, 1930s. The idea was scrapped after it was realised that there was insufficient car ownership in the city.

The Lucas stand at the Copenhagen Exhibition, 1935. The general consensus was that this was the most attractive and impressive st
in the entire motor section.

HRH the Prince of Wales leaving the Lucas stand at the Copenhagen Exhibition, 1935.

as Territorials marching towards Moor Street station, Birmingham, 1939.

as Territorials before the start of the Second World War.

as searchlight company, 1939.

TO write a Christmas Message this year is not easy—for much of the festive atmosphere that should surround this season is lacking due to the war. But as we have sent a Message of Greeting to our Employees and Trade Friends at home and overseas through the medium of our House Journal in other years we want to do so now — more especially as this issue of " Reflections " will be sent to every Lucas Employee who is serving with H.M. Forces.

Our message this year is one of encouragement. Some of you may read this in the front line, in a man o' war or in a well-camouflaged aerodrome, others at the Works or in their homes. Wherever it reaches you we send you Hearty Greetings. In the ordinary way we look back on a year that is ending, recalling pleasant things as well as the more difficult ones ; but nowadays in a tangled world of international confusion we look forward. And we anticipate 1940 not only with renewed vigour and determination to complete that to which we have set our hands, but also in the firm conviction that we shall emerge from the conflict victorious. Let us then be encouraged and our will strengthened to complete the task ahead of us. The following immortal words of Shakespeare seem to us very appropriate at the present time :—

> Come the three corners of the world in arms
> And we shall shock them. Naught shall make us rue
> If England to itself do rest but true.

Christmas comes but once a year and it is a season when we think of others. While thanking our Employees of all grades for their continued loyalty — a fact of which we are always mindful — we remember our Agents at Home and Overseas and when paying tribute to their efforts during the last year we want them to know that we are still the same Lucas trying to do a job of work.

And so with 1939 rapidly receding let us with courage in our hearts face the dawn of 1940.

Peter F. Bennett

Oliver Lucas.

The Christmas message from Oliver Lucas, 1939.

Soldiers of the 381st Company on active service during the Second World War.

CHAPTER FIVE

Health & Safety

Various health and safety acts over the years meant that Lucas had to provide adequate facilities for taking care of its workforce. In 1917 there was no company doctor, not even a nurse was on hand – all there would have been was a first aid box in the clocking-in office. As time went on the company was required to appoint a member of the workforce from each shop for putting on bandages. First aid was always done in the clocking-in offices.

An ambulance room was opened at Great King Street in 1920, but with 3,000 employees on site the single nurse who staffed it must have been woefully overstretched. When nightshifts were being worked an extra nurse would be on hand and a doctor would make infrequent visits to this and other sites. Lucas had a Welfare Officer who would make home visits to those who were off work ill, and he, in turn, reported to the Welfare Committee. It was not until 1924 that the company appointed a Safety Officer. The reports for that year indicate that company-wide there were 580 accidents and 605 illnesses.

Lucas made an endowment of two beds at the Queen Elizabeth Hospital and two at the General in 1925. In making financial donations Lucas expected some return, of course: if there was a serious accident, for example, they hoped to have priority on 'their' beds. On the other hand, though, it must be stressed that the company was a generous benefactor to many good causes. In 1927 Bertram Waring instigated the setting up of rest homes for women. The first of these was to be located at Weston-super-Mare. A new dental room was built and a full-time dentist was employed at Formans Road battery factory.

In due course safety guards was fitted to machinery in the factories in an attempt to minimise the number of accidents which occurred. But even after this the 1930 medical records show that the company lost some 39,348 working hours through accidents or staff attending the ambulance room for wound dressing.

When Lucas built a new block on the corner of Great King Street and Well Street, they decided to add a medical facility. This paved the way for a new approach to medical services in the company: full-time doctors and nurses replaced part-time medical staff and free dentistry was made available to all workers.

By the 1970s the company's south Birmingham factories were served by Senior Medical Officer Dr McCormack, affectionately known as 'Dr Mac'. He remained at Lucas for twenty-nine years until his retirement in 1977.

Dr Mac qualified at University College, Dublin, joined the RAF in 1940, and served until 1947 when he was demobilised. With Lucas he covered the Formans Road and Shaftmoor Lane sites, but following the growth of the company, this was extended to include Girling at Tyseley and Group Research at Monkspath in Solihull.

A gathering of Lucas employe with Dr Mac, left of centre, ne to the man in the white apro

'Dr Mac' at one of the many presentations held in his honour. Dr Mac was a keen supporter of ru A good player in his day, he was a one-time President of the Lucas rugby club. He was also an extremely w respected member of the Lucas family.

er Beryl Jones at
Cranmore Works,
71. As the only
se on site, life was
y busy for Beryl.
e security staff at
nmore were all
ned first-aiders,
hat provided her
h some degree of
pport.

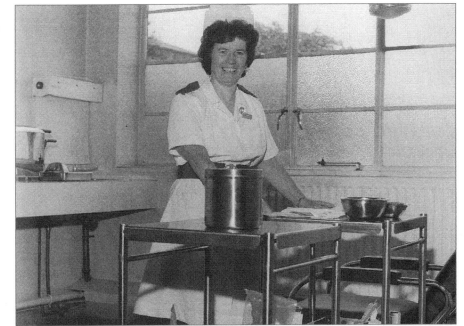

er Beryl Jones at the retirement gathering held for George Walker at Cranmore, late 1970s. Sister Beryl
red in 1982, although she returned to Lucas Marshall Lake Road from time to time as an agency nurse to
er holidays.

"INWOOD"

comes of age

HOW many of you realize that it is now 21 years since "Inwood" was opened by the Company as a Rest Home for women. Its new and beautiful baby brother "Eastern House" makes it feel a little conscious of the passing of the years— many of them war years, but it is soon to be subjected to various alterations and renovations and then will fear no comparisons.

Many of you know the Matron, Miss E. Pixton, whose charm and care has done much to restore you to good health. Every year a surprising number of women who have been with the Company for years and years venture to "Inwood" for the first time and then cannot think why they have not made use of the home before.

"Inwood" is provided by the Company for those who are in need of convalescence following an illness or operation or in need of a rest to avoid a breakdown. If this applies to you see your foreman and apply to your Personnel Assistant or to the Personnel Department for an application form. Both your foreman and your own Doctor, or the Works Medical Officer, must sign the form before your application can be considered by the women members of the Rest Homes Advisory Committee.

There are certain regulations about service, etc. which, if you do not fulfil, means that your application will have to be very specially considered and may even be rejected. Your foreman can give you the details.

You probably know the Rest Homes Advisory Committee is a sub-committee of the Central Joint Production Committee and consists of five men and women elected by the C.J.P.C. each year and three nominated members of the management. But to return to "Inwood"—

The house is beautifully situated on the hills overlooking Weston and Breen Down to Uphill and Bridgewater Bay. The woods come down to the garden at the back of the house, which is pleasantly shady in the summer. There are attractive rooms, a wireless and a piano and most comfortable beds. There is also central heating so it is nice and warm at this time of the year, and in any case Weston is much milder than 'Brum', and already there are a number of spring flowers out. For those who are interested, Matron has a guidebook and is always ready to suggest pleasant outings, long or short. The town has good shops and Matron manages to provide plenty of food, because everyone always gets hungry there. And we must not forget the parties to welcome new patients and bid farewell to the old ones.

Remember there are nearly always vacancies in the spring and autumn and it is at this time of the year you get colds and feel run down, so think of "Inwood" which gives you an opportunity to convalesce for two weeks. Therefore if you are genuinely under the weather ask your Personnel Department.

A happy party in the window of the sun lounge.

Matron chats with Miss Faulkner (Right 49 years' service and still with us).

opening of the Eastern House men's rest
ne in Weston-super-Mare, 1948.

osite: Inwood opened in about 1932.
s article appeared in *Reflections, c.* 1953.

retirement of Sister Swift (centre), Shaftmoor
e, *c.* 1969. Dr Mac stands next to her. Among
others in this photograph are Dr Aston, Chief
lical Officer for the Group, Sister Elizabeth
Fall, Chief Nursing Officer, Sister Mary
ars, Sister Val Baldwin, and other nursing
at Shaftmoor Lane.

Official opening of
MEN'S REST HOME

AN interesting ceremony took place on Saturday, 23rd October, 1948, when our Chairman, Sir Peter Bennett, M.P., opened Eastern House, Weston-super-Mare, the Rest Home for men.

Eastern House has been purchased from funds set aside for the welfare of our workers and modernised and equipped to meet the needs of those male employees who require a period of rest or recuperation. The decorations and furnishings are all in excellent taste and combine to give just that touch of cheerful homeliness which is so essential.

In a speech of welcome to the visitors Sir Peter Bennett recalled the days of long ago when welfare work and social amenities for the workers were unknown. He briefly reviewed the gradual improvements in conditions which had led to the establishing of sports grounds with their facilities for all kinds of recreation, the opening of "Inwood", our Home for women and girls, and now the acquisition of Eastern House for the use of the men.

Sir Peter went on to explain that a Home for the men would have been in operation earlier had it not been for the rearmament programme in 1938 and the war in 1939. In its original state Eastern House was anything but ideal for the job in mind, but by the efforts of our Works Engineer, Mr. L. R. Perkins, and the men of his department, it had been completely transformed He cited the bowling green at the rear of the house which but a few months ago was an asphalt playground and mentioned that the summer house overlooking the green had once belonged to the 'Old Guvnor' (the late Mr. Harry Lucas) and had stood in the garden of his home at Birmingham.

A going-away gathering for Sister McFall, Shaftmoor Lane, 1980s.

Sister Val Baldwin with Sister Ann Richardson holding Val's new baby Sarah, 1970s. Also shown are Si
McFall, Dr Mac, Dr Beattie and Sister Mary Shears.

CHAPTER SIX

Group Research Centre

U ntil the Lucas Research Centre was set up in Shirley, Solihull, small research departments operated in various factories across the company. As time passed, though, the demanding research programme that was required outgrew these slightly ad hoc facilities – hence the Research Centre.

The foyer and reception area of Lucas Group Research Centre.

An aerial shot of the Lucas Group Research Centre, 1965.

Dale Evans and Mandy Buckley, receptionists. They would have, at one time, welcomed you to Lucas: now TRW.

ting the structural strength of metal, 1980s.

in Anderson and Colin Gregory in the office, 987.

Colin Gregory hard at work, 1987.

FAREWELL TO DOCTOR ARROL

Director of Group Research Retires

Dr William J. Arroll retired as the director of Group Research at the end of the year after 23 years with Lucas.

Dr Arrol's career before joining Lucas was varied and interesting. After graduating at London University in 1935 he carried out research both at Imperial College and Oxford before joining the RNVR in 1940 as a radar officer. After service at sea in cruisers he was transferred—unusual in wartime—to a civilian post in Canada which turned out to be the setting up of the British part of the nuclear programme in Montreal in 1943. At the end of the war he returned to this country and became a lecturer at London University until 1948 when he went to Harwell for five years.

In 1953, Dr. Arrol joined the Electrical Company as research manager but for two years no laboratory existed. The first laboratory at Great King Street was on E8 and was soon found to be too small for the increasing staff. Sir Bertram Waring then appointed Dr Arrol director of group research and the build-up phase of the Group Research Centre began in two temporary buildings behind the Marston Green factory. These too, rapidly became too small for the developing organisation and finally in 1965 the present building at Shirley came into operation. Today the Lucas Group Research Centre has a high reputation both in this country and overseas.

It has always been a matter of satisfaction to Dr Arrol that so many people have joined the Group Research Centre staff and later passed across to Lucas companies in one or other managerial capacity and that several of them now occupy very senior posts indeed.

Dr Arrol has been well-known as an industrial research director and from 1970 to 1973 was President of the European Industrial Research Management Association. His chief recreation since boyhood has been sailing and this will continue after his retirement.

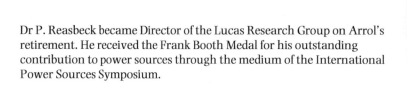

Dr P. Reasbeck became Director of the Lucas Research Group on Arrol's retirement. He received the Frank Booth Medal for his outstanding contribution to power sources through the medium of the International Power Sources Symposium.

ila Gilbert and Joan Moorcroft mixing
micals as part of the complex analytical
earch which was undertaken at the
earch Centre, 1982.

Some of the staff of the Research Centre on a night out, 1985. Seen here are M. Denby, John Mackintosh, Garritty, Graham Johnson and Brian Norway.

Above: One of the research staff; unfortunately his name not known. In the 1980s about 250 people worked on site.

Left: Bob James, a research chemist, 1978.

CHAPTER SEVEN

Personalities

The dictionary describes a personality as someone with a distinctive character. Singling out just a few of the many personalities at Lucas is a difficult task, as so many of the company's employees are worthy of inclusion.

Jack Smith represented Lucas during the 1930s and '40s. He is remembered today as a tough character, as those who got on the wrong side of him will testify, but he was always a fair man, and always willing to get involved in Great King Street activities.

Bill Harley was a completely different character. A sound and well-respected supervisor, his forte was organising and motivating his staff. Bill was involved in a whole host of activities outside work, especially his beloved bowls.

I have known Marge Summerfield for over forty years, since she joined the BW5 gas turbine factory in about 1963. She was always in the forefront of the factory's social life, much involved in the organisation of children's and pensioners' parties, for example. Her love of life is immeasurable.

JACK SMITH
Great King Street General Manager Jack Smith. When he retired on 18 June 1949 he received a television set from the Chairman, Lord Peter Bennett. It was said that Jack was a hard man, but he always got the job done, and earned great respect from his colleagues as a result.

Jack Smith.

A keen bowls player, Jack is seen here with other members of the Lucas Bowling Club, 1930s.

Jack at the bowls club, 1930s.

Jack shakes hands with the winning captain at a Lucas cricket match, 1930s.

ing his goodbyes to friends and eagues from Lucas Great King Street, 9.

BILL HARLEY

In August 1987, after thirty-one years' loyal service, seventeen of which were spent on the nightshift, Bill Harley retired. He had joined the company as a patrol viewer in G2 Autos, but quickly moved through the ranks as a charge-hand, then a foreman. His wife Alice, his sister and other family members have also worked at Lucas.

During his time with the company Bill found time to take a prominent part in the social scene at Great King Street. He was a founder member of the Production Supervisors' Association and of the Lucas branch of the British Legion. Endlessly active, Bill was also Social Secretary of the Bowls Club, and in 1977 he organised the Birmingham Lucas Horticultural Society. Word now has it that he has taken up organising Latin American dancing! Is there no end to his interests and talents?

Bill Harley in 1987.

It seems the entire department turned out for the retirement gathering held for Bill on 12 July 1987.

Bill bids a fond farewell to fellow nightshift supervisors at Great King Street, 1987.

Bill in his younger days, receiving a trophy for bowling from General Factories Manager Reg Leach, 1960.

Bowls Club Ladies' Night, *c.* 1960. Among those attending the dance are, back row, left to right: Tom Jaru Bill Harley, Tom Harley, George Saving, Jack Manning. Front row: Eva Jarus, Rose Harley, Mrs Saving, M Manning and Alice Harley.

Lucas colleagues and their wives attending a formal event, 1960s. Bi is standing on the left.

MARGE SUMMERFIELD

I first got to know Marge Summerfield (née Benton) in 1963 when she came up to BW5 Gas Turbine, Shaftmoor Lane, from Great King Street. There was no way you could miss Marge with her bubbly, energetic personality. But it was not this which endeared her to me, but the sheer kindness and willingness she displayed in helping others. Marge was a member of Wal Bradbury's team of hospital volunteers – these people gave up many hours to spend time at the hospital. She was also heavily involved in organising events for pensioners and children, and gave much of her own time to many other just causes.

In 1983 Marge decided to retire, and when her final day of work came she received the biggest and best send-off perhaps ever given for a Lucas employee. Countless friends and colleagues turned out to show their appreciation for all she had done over the years. Sadly, life has a knack of being unkind, and shortly after Marge's retirement her dear husband Wilf suffered a major stroke, which left him requiring round-the-clock care. Despite her own battle with arthritis, Marge takes care of Wilf and still remains a very bubbly personality, always willing to put others before herself even to this day. She is truly a unique lady.

Arthur Middleton, Factory Manager at Lucas BW5 Shaftmoor Lane, gives Marge Summerfield a friendly hug on the day of her retirement, 1983.

So many people turned out to wish Marge well on her last day that two photographs had to be taken! General Foreman Mike Rogers presented her with flowers.

CHAPTER EIGHT

Hilver

Hilver became the home of Harry Lucas and his family in 1898. The original lamp company had been doing rather well and Harry was a firm believer in rewards for hard work done. Doubtless the acquisition of such a property would have meant that the Lucas family had 'arrived'. The name 'Hilver' was a hybrid of the Christian names of Harry's two children: Hilda and Oliver.

Most Lucas employees will remember Hilver in its guise as a training establishment, but it was not the first. Way back, the first training venue was a house at Primrose Hill which was originally owned by the Cadbury family. The company had always recognised the benefit of training, but for the most part this was for supervisors and foremen and those higher up in the organisation's structure. It was quickly realised that training was the way forward and that the Primrose Hill site would not be large enough to cope with Lucas's growing needs. Lucas began to implement a first-class training system for all employees, and to this end had to acquire more venues to accommodate them.

Hilver became the Lucas Residential Instruction Centre in 1952, and around this time the company also acquired property at 7 and 9 St Agnes Road, Moseley. Of course these were not the only training locations: many Lucas girls will recall the Nissen hut at Shaftmoor Lane, where they received instruction before being allowed on to the factory floor.

At Hilver there were many different courses on offer. Some lasted a day or two, others a whole week or a fortnight. The training centre was also used to accommodate long-term courses. It was widely acknowledged that Lucas supplied some of the best industrial education facilities for its workforce in the whole of the United Kingdom.

In the late 1990s, when the announcement of the closure of Lucas came, the decision was made to sell off the company's training establishments. They were auctioned off as private dwellings. Sir Kumar Bhattacharyya, perhaps the most influential manufacturing industry expert in the UK, and also a Lucas man, bought Hilver.

Hilda and Oliver Lucas, after whom Hilver was named.

Attendees at a supervisors' course at Hilver in the 1960s. These men would have come from Lucas factories all over the country: from Liverpool, Burnley and Sudbury as well as from the various branches in the Midlands.

The very name
St Agnes Road will
bring back many
memories of Hilver to
those who attended
training courses there.

Hilver, formerly the home of Harry Lucas and his family, during the years when it was used to accommodate company training facilities.

The rear of the Hilver establishment featuring the elegant conservatory and well-tended gardens.

Nos 7 and 9 St Agnes Road,
Moseley. Along with Hilver, these
two properties housed Lucas's
training facilities.

The reception and hallway at Hilver.

Below: Some of the staff at Hilver in the 1980s. Seen here are Roy Harrington, Sue Page, Yvonn Wellings, Ann Stretton, Elizabeth Freston, Kath Reading, Jill Chippendale and Chris Stevens.

Students at Hilver tucking into a meal in the dining room.

Hilver staff, *c.* 1978.

The dining room set out for breakfast.

The Covered Wagon, first opened in 1962, was a popular watering hole for students at Hilver.

Nat and Brenda Gould with their son Simon. The couple were licensees of the Covered Wagon between 198
and 1999.

CHAPTER NINE

Lucas Reflections

Reflections was the name of the quarterly company magazine. It had something of interest for employees from all sections of the organisation, but in truth the magazine was a vehicle for fostering the family spirit for which Lucas is famous. It published not only company news, but went from factory to factory gathering 'people' news in a feature called 'Roundabout'. The magazine would have news of weddings, anniversaries and retirements, as well as results and features from Lucas's many sports clubs and news from the thriving social scene. Pensioners' and children's parties, events and occurrences from all across the company – everything you could wish to know about what was going on in Lucas was there.

Oliver Lucas was an advocate of this form of cross-company communication. He felt it was an extremely important tool which allowed Lucas employees to express themselves as well as getting information about the company to the employees. In effect, news was flowing up as well as down.

FOR PRIVATE CIRCULATION

LUCAS REFLECTIONS

TO HELP · TO INSTRUCT · TO INTEREST · TO ENCOURAGE

No. 1   July 1929.

FOREWORD

From the earliest days in the career of Joseph Lucas Limited, willing co-operation and assistance has been given by all employees, and their loyalty and devotion to duty has encouraged us in critical and anxious times. The prominent position which the Company now occupies in the industrial world, is a monument to their zeal and energy.

This result has been largely due to the aims and ideals of the Company, from the commencement of its activities, being imparted to its employees by personal contact with the Management, and the fundamental basis of these aims has been to foster the "team spirit".

Much as we desire to be personally in touch with all our people, the rapid growth and present size of the Organisation renders this increasingly difficult, and it has become necessary to search for a supplementary method of imparting our views and encouragement to every individual.

At the present time the Company has at heart the welfare of some 12,500 people; each one individually weak to withstand the blows of present day conditions, but collectively should be strong enough to withstand the most violent attack. It is vital that all employees realise, whilst the methods adopted in any business organisation are governed by the surrounding economic conditions of its industry, its stability can only be maintained by the co-operation of all its members. Competition tends to increase rather than to diminish, so improved efficiency of working and greater individual effort must be resorted to.

Every man or woman must do his or her share; each feeling that the effort is needed, not only because of personal comfort and gain, but for the well-being of their fellow workers by enabling the Company to ensure constant employment and good working conditions.

Slackness not only demoralises the individual, but causes unrest and may be disaster to yourself and those working around you. Thus the cultivation of the "team spirit" must be an ever prominent aim, as unless this ideal can be realised your own progress will be retarded. We want all our people to be real workers, working cheerfully and gladly, realising the difficulties that are being experienced and combining with the Management to overcome them.

The older members of our Organisation know the Company has grown to its present dimensions only by the hard work and hard thinking in the past by the Operatives, the Staff, and the Management. We desire that the younger people should give serious thought to the fact that the position held by the firm at the present did not just happen but had to be won and must be upheld by hard work and "team spirit".

In a search for some means to foster this "team spirit" in the altered conditions of the present day, we believe a solution is to be found in producing some form of internal publication which will not only impart our views, but will have items of interest to everyone in the different sections of the organisation. Hence the first number of "Reflections" comes into being.

P.F B.

O.L.

62.79.M   PRINTED & PUBLISHED BY JOSEPH LUCAS LIMITED, BIRMINGHAM, ENGLAND.

The first ever issue of *Reflections*, July 1929. The foreword was written by Peter Bennett and Oliver Lucas, who were at the time joint Managing Directors.

A MESSAGE FROM H.R.H. THE DUKE OF YORK

We are honoured to publish a message from H.R.H. The Duke of York to our readers. As is well-known, His Royal Highness takes a keen interest in industrial problems and frequently visits factories to see things for himself. His letter evincing his interest in Works and Staff Magazines will be read with great pleasure by readers of our magazine.

145 PICCADILLY
W.1.

December, 1935.

I hope you will convey to your readers my very best wishes for a prosperous New Year.

As President of the Industrial Welfare Society I receive quite a number of Works and Staff Magazines and I am very much impressed with the part they play in bringing together the members of Firms publishing them.

The creation of better understanding between men will, I hope, lead some day to better understanding between Nations, and I believe Works and Staff Magazines are performing a very useful work in this direction.

Albert

Message from HRH the Duke of York, 1935.

The front cover of the December 1939 issue of *Reflections*.

A list of *Reflections* correspondents from all over the Lucas organisation, 1970s.

Announcements of births, weddings and anniversaries from *Reflections*, 1982.

Congratulations

Correspondents

GT. KING STREET.
ALLEN, MISS E., Powers Room.
ALLEN, MR. JACK, K.6.
ADAMS, MISS DOROTHY, GK.3. Panel Line.
ADAMS, MR. H., R.3. Toolroom.
ARCHER, MR. C. F., R.5.
BAILEY, MR. H., Works Accounts.
BROOKES, MR., K.4. Tool Maintenance.
BECKETT, MR. L., K.5./G.5.
BAGSHAW, MR. H., A.4. Gauge Room.
BOSWORTH, MISS A., 'B' Block.
BAKER, MISS M., Personnel.
BARBOUR, MR. F., G.6.
CARR, MR. F., Staff Garage.
COXON, MR. W. Millwrights.
CROSS, MR. J. B., 'B' Block.
CARTER, MR. M. S., A.2. Customers' Returns.
DAWES, MR. S., M.6.
DRAYCOTT, MR. G., H.3.
FRENCH, MISS H., Pricing.
GRACE, MRS. J. F. E., M.6.D.O.
GRIFFITH, MR., Catering Dept., S. Block.
HALL, MISS F., Works Engineers' Office.
HARRIS, MR. G. W., H.4./G.4.
JACKSON, MR. T., GK.2. Stores.
JOYCE, MR. H., Cost Office, M.5.
MOORE, MISS ETHEL, Buying Dept.
PICKMAN, MR. J., R.6.
PARKER, MR. F., K.1. Plating, GK.2. Polishing.
REEVES, MISS E., Wages.
SHELTON, MISS A., Secretarial.
SIMMS, MR. H., Stationery.
SMITH, MISS IVY, K.3.
SPENCER, MISS E., General Office, M.3.
TAYLOR, MRS., Cleaners.
USHERWOOD, MR. S., G.2. Auto.
WATKINS, MR., M.4.
WANKLING, MR. H. C., R.5.

GT. HAMPTON STREET.
BRADLEY, G. A., Sales Ledger.
BREWER, MR. A. E., Trade School (Boys).
BROWN, MR. A., M.P.D.
SEAL, MR. J., Commercial Dept.
SMITH, MR. G., C.D.E.2.
TROMAN, MISS A., B.3.

SHAFTMOOR LANE.
ANSCOMBE, MR. G., B.W.3.
DEELEY, MR. E., B.W.4.
POSTLE, MR. S., Eng. and Development.
ROE, MR. R., General Office.
TEAGUE, MR. R. L., B.W.3.
WALKER, MR. R. W., B.W.4.A.
WILDING, MISS D., B.W.4.
WALLISS, MRS. M., General Office.

SPRING ROAD, TYSELEY.
HADLEY, MISS H.

EDITOR

Miss J. A. Parkes, Great King Street. All communications and contributions should be handed to departmental correspondents, or passed direct to the Editor. No anonymous communications will be published. Here is a list of your departmental correspondents:

FORMANS ROAD.
BULLEN, MR. F., Transport.
HOME, MISS ELLA, Transport.
HOWELLS, MRS. L., Batteries.
MILLINGTON, MISS.
MOUNTFORD, MISS I., Diecasting and Bakelite.
ROBERTS, MR. T. C., Toolroom.
WALKER, MR. S., Engineers' Maintenance.

P. & H.
ADKINS, MR. W. E., Top Floor.
CLARIDGE, MR. N., Central Floor.
CLARKE, MR. S., Sports and Social.
DOUBLEDAY, MR. H. E., Ground Floor.
HEYS, MR. G. B., P.C.D. Staff.

ROCKY LANE.
WALKER, MISS J.

MERE GREEN.
CLEMENTS, MR. J.

BURNLEY.
WOOD, MISS D. M., Personnel.
LLOYD, MR. F. S., Cost Office, Hargher Clough.
SCOTT, MR. C. B., M.P.D., Wood Top.
FAGAN, MR. J., Machine Shop, Wood Top.
WEIR, MR. W., P.C.D., Wood Top.

GARRISON LANE.
REEVES, MR. O., Stock Control.

LUCAS EBONITE.
DICKSON, MR. K. A.
HENSMAN MRS. K. E.

Births

Barnes. To Roy (toolroom Great King Street) and Ingrid, a daughter, Charlene Nicole, on 25 May 1982.

Dunn. To John (PED Shaftmoor Lane) and Christine (buying York Road) a son, Christopher Michael, on 21 September 1982.

Knight. To Raymond (works engineers Fradley) and Jean, a son, Marcus, on 20 September 1982.

Priddy. To Alan (PED Shaftmoor Lane) and Deborah, a son, David James, on 31 May 1982.

Weddings

Bennett. Martin (parts recall Fradley) to Amanda at All Saints' Church, Alrewas, on 30 October 1982.

Brittain-Greening. Roger (Reflections Great King Street) to Karen at Birmingham Register Office, on 7 October 1982.

Bladon-Johnson. Vince (Hanger 5 Fradley) to Lesley (Hanger 5 Fradley) at St John The Baptist Church, Armitage on 16 October 1982.

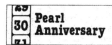

Pearl Anniversary

Tobone-Attard. Tony (Formans Road) to Mary (retired from Formans Road) at St John's Catholic Church, Balsall Heath, on 20 December 1952.

Caroline Graham (PED BW5 Shaftmoor Lane), on 8 September 1982.

Chris Grice (management services Shaftmoor Lane), on 4 October 1982.

Kay Jones (buying office BW5 Shaftmoor Lane), on 29 October 1982.

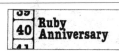

Ruby Anniversary

Page. Elsie (retired from Marshall Lake Road) to Arthur at St John's Church, Birmingham, on 7 October 1942.

Taylor-Meaton. Gwen (retired from BW3 Shaftmoor Lane) to Ken at St Paul's Church, on 5 December 1942.

A photograph which appeared in *Reflections* of the wedding of Frederick Poole and Edna Jones, which took place on 18 June 1949 at Yardley Wood parish church. Edna's father was Oliver Lucas's chauffeur.

Below: A pensions article penned by Tony Gill, 1993.

The Lucas Pension Scheme

Reflections

Issue No 4 December 1993 A newsletter for Lucas Pensioners

Souvenir Commemorative Issue

65 1928 – 1993 Years of Lucas Pensions

Tony Gill

A message from the Chairman

Lucas started its first pension scheme sixty five years ago on 1 July 1928 and I am pleased to have been asked to write an introduction to this commemorative edition of *Reflections*. Within pensions, sixty five has a special meaning; it is the age by which most people have retired. A pension scheme, however, does not retire when it has been in existence for sixty five years. Indeed, the Lucas Pension Scheme is becoming responsible now for future commitments – some of which will continue after another sixty five years have passed.

In the 1920s the fear of poverty in old age was still very largely the scourge it had been in the nineteenth century. The first Lucas pension arrangement was the vision of two men: Lord Bennett and Sir Bertram Waring. Each of them later became the Lucas Chairman. It was their initiative and planning that led to the scheme being set up. Both desired Lucas to have a scheme that would provide a long serving employee with a pension that would take away the dread of old age.

I am pleased the Pensions Department has produced this special issue of *Reflections* to commemorate the launching of the scheme and to detail the labours of Peter Bennett, Bertram Waring and their colleagues on behalf of Lucas employees.

Chapter Ten
Advertising

dvertising is a powerful force, and Lucas spent millions to bring its products to the attention of the general public; in the Birmingham area its name appeared on hoardings and even on the backs of buses. It also advertised in the trade press, gave away promotional products and even built its own private suite at the NEC for use at trade fairs. Today many of the old adverts and slogans have nostalgic value, but the reasons for some of the specialised trade advertisements are lost in the mists of time!

Lucas – 'King of the Road': the company's first logan, used for many years. The phrase 'Use Lucas Cyclealities' didn't catch on!

An early advertisement for Lucas Trafficators, whe[n] flashing indicators had yet to be invented.

A Lucas batteries advertisement from 1935.

1930s radio battery advertising campaign with £100 competition tie-in.

This is the last month of the C.A.V. Radio Battery Contest, and we hope that all our Agents are in the midst of the "big push." No effort should be spared to make this Competition a huge success, the greater its success more business for the Agents, and the deciding factor as to whether the Competition is a success or not in any district is the local Agent.

□ □ □

The closing date is March 29th, but before then there is time to double previous efforts.

Here is a photograph of our window at Great Hampton Street, drawing attention to the C.A.V. Radio Battery Contest. We hope that our Agents have an equally attractive window.

BATTERY AGENTS' SECTION

Published to Further the Interests of all
LUCAS-C.A.V.-ROTAX Battery Service Agents
& Spares Stockists.

A 1952 advert featuring Lucas lamps through the ages.

'Metal matters': a typical advertisement from the trade press, which associates the name of Lucas with metal in many forms.

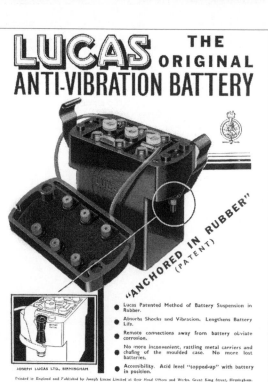

Above: A Lucas battery was considered to be reliable and one of the best. Today we forget what it was like when batteries weren't sealed, and needed topping up – especially in the winter.

This anti-vibration battery advert lists the battery's benefits in detail.

very innovation used to be advertised in great
detail – a far cry from today's strong visual images
with minimal text.

Above: A trade advert that draws the attention of
retailers to the range of Lucas promotional material
that was available.

Another trade advertisement that highlights some of
the applications of Lucas products.

"I'm sorry too. Thank goodness I don't have to bother about greasing nowadays—I always hated it!"

"Getting lazy and neglectful in your old age, I suppose?"

"No, just Luvax-Bijur, that's all. It's entirely automatic and built into the chassis as part of the design. Saves you all that trouble and mess, and does the job miles better, too!"

The Luvax-Bijur system ensures that every vital chassis point is continually, *automatically* fed with oil (the finest lubricant), varied by the car itself to the correct amount to suit different running conditions. You get greater ease of control and safety, more silent running, greater driving comfort and peace of mind, and minimum wear, deterioration and maintenance cost. The sole attention required is occasional refilling of the oil reservoir.

Write for interesting illustrated folder giving full details, from Joseph Lucas Ltd., Birmingham, 19.

LUVAX-BIJUR
Automatic CHASSIS LUBRICATION
SUPPLIED & SERVICED BY JOSEPH LUCAS LTD.

A Lucas advertisement that reminds us of the days when cars needed much more servicing.

CHAPTER ELEVEN

Out & About

Lucas's *Reflections* magazine used to carry a regular item entitled 'Out and About', which included news from the various factory correspondents. I have used this title for this chapter, which takes us on a tour round some of Lucas's factories, illustrated with some of the photographs that have kindly been sent to me by ex-Lucas employees.

A group of Lucas ladies from all over the country – Sudbury, Cwmbran, Liverpool, Acton, Burnley, as well as Midlands factories. Among those seen here are Gertie James, Winnie Kennard, Mabel Dudley, Violet Hemmings, Nancy Davies, Kitty Glasgow, Ruth Lynch, A. Buttrey, E. Humphries, Mary Caldicott, Hilda Spicer, Doris Naylor, Phyllis Bryant, Dorothy Moore, Margaret Kenny and Ellen McGuire. The motto of these ladies is as follows: 'We make new friends, we keep the old, Some are silver, some are gold, Brows may wrinkle, hair go grey, But real friendships will never decay.'

GREAT KING STREET
I would like to think that many ex-employees will recognise themselves, or people that they know in the following photographs.

An unusual photograph of ladies at a lunchtime dance, possibly on the roof of Great King Street, 1930s.

Below: A group of Lucas Great King Street ladies about to head off on a coach trip to London, 1950s.

certificate of apprenticeship awarded to Robert
Morris, who learned his trade at Great King Street
during the 1950s.

on Thomas operating a B4 milling machine at
Great King Street, 1961.

The GK3
Flashers, 1963

Great King Street Manager Bob Milburn presents a rather ornate clock to Edgar Shell on the occasion of h
retirement in December 1965.

ob Milburn presenting gifts to Cyril Hopkins on his retirement from Lucas in 1965.

ederick Bolton makes a presentation to Tudor Jones on his retirement in 1981.

Harold Riches was Lucas's Father Christmas. Here he is with
employees' children during the 1970s.

ay Whelan, a Supervisor at Great King Street, makes a presentation to a member of staff, 1970s.

hil Barrington chairs the Great King Street Children's Party Committee, early 1980s. Eric Merryweather is
eated on the far right.

Roy Barlow, General Factories Manager, wishes Harold Riches and Jack Edwards all the best from B Block on their retirement, *c*. 1980.

Roy Barlow makes a presentation to Edna Hanson on the occasion of her retirement, 1980.

Doug Waltham presents Norman Walker with gifts to commemorate his fifty years' loyal service to Lucas, April 1980.

The staff of K5 Distributors raised money to buy toys for the children's hospice Orchardside, 1970s.

Tom Gannon bids a fond farewell to Ron Aston, who retired in April 1983. Also in the photograph are Vic Smith, Stan Leyton and Eric Merryweather.

John Linforth, General Manager of Great King Street, explains working practices to Lt Col Brook-Johnson, City Serjeant-at-Arms (London). John was given the unwelcome task of closing the Great King Street works in the mid-1990s, and moving production out to other sites.

SHAFTMOOR LANE
The group of factories on this site stretched across Spring Road. Over 8,000 people were employed in BW3 (dynamo and starter), BW4 (lamp factory) and No. 5 factory (gas turbine, later aerospace).

The shop floor of the Bakelite production department bedecked with bunting and flags on George VI's Coronation day, 1937.

Below: Mr Smith, Factory Manager at BW4, presents Foreman Mr Benson with gifts on his retirement in 1958. Jack Nicholls (in the white coat) looks on.

foremen's reunion dinner, 1947. Adrian Hewitt is second from the right in the front row. Eric Cowton, second from the left in the front row, went on to become Factory Manager at BW4.

must have been Frank Morris's lucky day! Here he is taking delivery of a brand new car, first prize in a Lucas raw, 1960s.

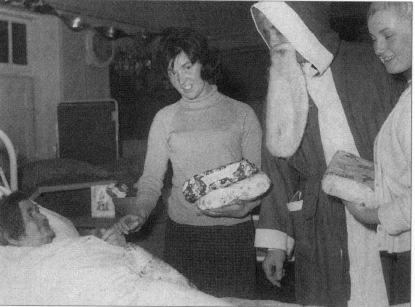

Above: Walter Bradbury, instigator of the hospital volunteers team, seen here with his wife (holdin bouquet), is presented with retirement gifts. Among those present are Edna Hawthorn, Cathy Wheeler, Dusty Bedwort Harry and Nellie Grove, Gordon Bunce, Evelyn Bedworth, George Thoma and Ken Walker.

The author making a hospital visit disguised as Father Christmas, 1960s Holding the gifts in the centre of the photograph is Evelyn Gill.

ucas BW5 ward visitors and nursing staff pose for a Christmas snapshot, 1960s. Among those in the photograph are Cathy Wheeler, Evelyn Gill, Mr and Mrs Walter Bradbury, Jack Gravenor, George Thomas and ordon Bunce.

ucas volunteers on one of the wards at Dudley Road Hospital, 1960s.

A presentation was made to Tony Hill from the Production Department at Spring Road on the occasion of h marriage, September 1970.

George Wilson, General Foreman of the Roller Clutch Department, presents wedding gifts to Connie Field o behalf of her friends, 1970s.

John Brett, Yoke Shop Foreman, wishes all the best to Joe Farmer, Superintendent, on his retirement, *c.* 1970.

Above: A leaving gathering for
~~~ean, 1962. Among those present
~ere Mary ?, Judy Porter, Mavis
~acy, Gordon Bunce, George Nash
~nd Edna Hawthorn.

A gathering on the occasion of
~om Jones's retirement, *c.* 1977.
~om spent his early working life
~s a miner in Wales, and even
~layed the trumpet in the colliery
~and. Here his Foreman Brian
~heppard presents him with a
~heque and wishes him well on
~ehalf of all his friends at BW5.
~mong those in the photograph
~re Ivor Slack, Albert Ashford,
~len Forder, Dave Brown, Geoff
~emberton, Dave Griffiths and
~lbert Mulliss.

Len Bevin and his wife at a formal dinner with Mr and Mrs Bert Evetts, Group Manufacturing Director. Len was born in 1927 and lived in Gee Street, Lozells, close to the Great King Street factory. When I was gathering material for this book I got into contact with Len, having known him from my days at BW5. He began at Lucas in 1941, at the same time as three other lads began their apprenticeships. They were Frank Smith, whose father worked in the tool room; Alan Jones, whose father was chauffeur to Sir Bertram Waring; and Charlie Turner. Len had many relations working in the Lucas organisation, among them two uncles, one in G4 and another in GK2 polishing shop. The information which he was able to pass on to me brought back many happy memories – it was like taking a step back in time.

Len Bevin and his wife meet Lucas Chairman Sir Bernard Scott.

The retirement
gathering for Bob
Aikens, *c.* 1980.
Among those pictured
here are Harold Jones,
Mrs Aikens, Ronnie
Naughton, Judy Peach,
Marge Summerfield and
Reg Peach.

Evelyn Gill checking
gears in the late
1970s.

FORDHOUSES, WOLVERHAMPTON

H.M. Hobson built this Wolverhampton factory and began the business with a twelve-strong workforce in June 1940. Originally they were employed on machining the AV70M carburettor bodies for Cheetah engines. Even after the end of the Second World War, there was still government demand for military equipment and components, so Hobson's was occupied with this well into peacetime. In 1970 the Lucas Group decided to launch a takeover for Hobson's and eventually purchased the company. It became part of the Actuation Division in 1973. The Fordhouses factory has seen many changes over the years and the name Lucas has now been replaced by that of Goodrich UK.

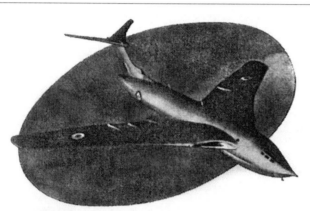

Hobson Power Controls

operate all the primary control surfaces on the

HANDLEY PAGE 'VICTOR'
BRITAIN'S FIRST CRESCENT WINGED BOMBER

HOBSON POWER FLYING CONTROLS are now being specified for a number of British aircraft including those incorporating "All flying" or "Slab" tailplanes.
The unit, as illustrated, is a self-contained duplicated electro-hydraulic screwjack type for operation of port or starboard ailerons.

H. M. HOBSON LIMITED
FORDHOUSES · WOLVERHAMPTON

Licensees in U.S.A.: Simmonds Aerocessories Inc., Tarrytown, NEW YORK, U.S.A.
Licensees in Italy : Secondo Mona, SOMMA LOMBARDO.
Agents in France : Societe Commerciale et Industrielle Franco-Britannique, 48 Avenue Raymond Poincare, PARIS XVI.

Agents in Australia: Aeronautical Supply Co. Pty. Ltd., 210 Victoria Street, MELBOURNE, Victoria.
Agents in Spain: Senor Ramon Bacario, Nunez de Balboa, 29, MADRID.
Agents in Egypt and Syria: T. G. Mapplebeck, 48, Sharia Abdel-Khalek Sarwat Pasha, CAIRO, Egypt.

Agents in Israel : Curt Israel, P.O.B. 1999, TEL AVIV.

An early piece of Hobson's advertising.

John Middlebrook, Supplies Manager, and Bernard Williams, Operations Manager at Fordhouses.

Bill Ganner, a Production Manager at Fordhouses from 1974 to 1986.

...aker Cup Final programme from 1973, when Hobson's
...ok on Goodyear.

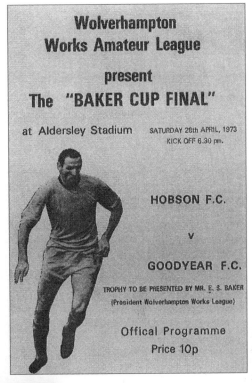

Hobson's players with the Baker
Cup after their victory in the
1990 final. Left to right: Sid Price,
Ken Bates and Wayne Roberts.

TERRY DUFFY was born in Wolverhampton in 1922 and on leaving school he was employed as a sheet metal worker until joining the Leicestershire Regiment as an infantryman at the age of seventeen. He had a distinguished military career, seeing service in Italy, North Africa, Greece and Austria, and rose to the rank of sergeant-major by the end of the Second World War. Terry began work at Hobson's in the mid-1950s as a machinist in the main machine shop. Interested in the Trade Union movement, Terry became an active member of the AEU and held senior positions on union committees.

By 1975 he had been elected on to the AEU Executive Council, and three years later he was chosen to become the union's National President.

His time at Hobson's is remembered for the way he motivated the shop stewards committee, brought recognition and respect to the movement, and how he obtained the best working conditions possible to the workforce. Terry sadly died in 1985, but he will long be remembered as a sincere and honest man of integrity.

Terry with Neil Kinnock and members of the AEU National Executive, early 1980s.

MARSHALL LAKE ROAD

Marshall Lake Road, in Shirley, was built for BSA in 1941 – to get the company out of central Birmingham, which at that time was being heavily bombed. BSA made guns there, and when Lucas took over in the 1970s the cellars used for testing the guns had to be filled in, so that it was safe to install heavy machinery.

Marshall Lake Road staff were forever raising money for good causes. Here, Dr Richard Stockdale receives a cheque for £900 for Birmingham Children's Hospital after his cross-Channel swim in the 1970s.

Assistant Factory Manager Jim Davidson does the honours at a retirement bash in the early 1980s. It looks as if almost all the Marshall Lake Road girls have turned out for this photograph!

Marshall Lake Road employees and friends on a trip to Paris in the 1970s.

Mike Lemon, General Manager at the starters and alternators factory, presents a gift to a retiring Engineering Foreman. Looking on are Gordon Bunce, Fred Schofield and Peter Hopkins.

Bill Morris, a well-respected Senior Fire and Security Officer at Marshall Lake Road receives a watch from Gordon Bunce on his retirement in 1982.

GREAT HAMPTON STREET
Great Hampton Street was situated only a short distance from Lucas's Great King Street factory. It housed the company parts and service department.

Friends say their farewells to Ann Forfitt on her last day at Great Hampton Street, 1980s.

departmental athering to say oodbye to Ann.

LUCAS ELECTRICAL COMPANY, CANNOCK

In 1950 Lucas predicted that the number of new motor vehicles in Britain would increase from about 27,000 a week to 46,000 by 1960. This would obviously have an effect on Lucas production levels, so the company built a factory north of Birmingham at Cannock in Staffordshire, to give itself much-needed extra capacity. This 100,000 sq. ft factory on a 19-acre site opened in 1956, employing mainly women on two shifts. Oil-filled ignition coils were the first items to be produced; later the factory became a major lamp manufacturer.

Unfortunately the car industry went into sharp decline in 1957, because of economic recession, which put paid to Lucas's expansion plans.

A Ladies *v.* Gentlemen novelty football match, held at Cannock in 1970 to raise funds for a kidney machine for the local hospital. The report in *Reflections* tells us that 'the ladies won and carried off the trophy in fine style'.

John William Cornwall began at the Lighting Division, Cannock, in 1960. He became a well-respected figure and a leading steward.

CHAPTER TWELVE

Lucas at Play

An active social life was an important part of working at Lucas in its heyday. Coach trips were very much the thing in the days before car ownership was so widespread. They were always a popular part of Lucas life, especially in factories where the workforce was primarily female. Added to this, there were huge numbers of sports teams that helped to keep the workforce fit and active, and a wide range of clubs and societies for hobbies and pastimes.

y Williams of Lucas Great King Street, seen here far right with her son, before boarding a coach bound for the estival of Britain, 1951. During the Second World War Joy recalls painting the glass in the windows of Great ing Street for the blackout. Lucas factories were a target for German bombers during the war.

Mrs Rayboul[
receives the
ladies' tug-of-
war trophy
from Mrs
Harry Lucas,
1930s.

A day out to
Brighton from
the Acton
factory, 1949

Ladies' Day at the Bowling Club had been a very popular event before the Second World War. This photograp
is of the first postwar Ladies' Day, July 1949. It was very well attended, with sixty people coming along to t
event at the Laurel Road bowling green.

A very tough bunch of boxers, on the occasion of the Lucas Challenge Cup Final, 1949. Among those seen here are G.H. Croggatt, A. Beard, W. Moorcroft, A. Freer, H. James, . Gleinitz, J. Wood nd S. Wright.

articipants in a fun run organised by Lucas Service to raise money for charity, 1970s.

The Central Toolroom football team, 1950. Len Bevin, Neville Lloyd, Seth Samuels, Barry Baker, Frank Penrose and referee Don Mainwaring can all be seen here.

Ken Marple and Harold Riches' son Larry fishing at Lucas Harvington Waters, 1964.

Lucas anglers at Elkington Water, 1961. Among those seen here are David Bourne, Vic Merryweather, Charlie Wilkinson, Frank Wells, Bill Powis, Harry Birchley, Bert Fife, Alan Elsmore, Ken Marple, Ernie Forty, Dave Paget and Albert Morgan.

ucas Society of Model Engineers held an event at Dudley Road Hospital on 7 September 1970. The train driver
ere is Norman Smith.

few members of the Lucas Society of Model Engineers. Left to right: Norman Hince, Ernie Homer, Wilf
ennett, Derek Allen, Ken Toone, Pat Morton, Robin ?, John Godfrey, Clive Slater, Norman Noakes.

John Armstrong, Director of Education of Lucas Industries tries his hand at model train driving, while Hen
Price looks on, 1972.

Members of the Lucas Railway Society at a model railway display, which was set up for charity.

CHAPTER THIRTEEN

Build Them Up

Over the years Lucas has seen its factory premises change dramatically. One could say that the demolition of the Great King Street factory was the most dramatic of all, and was perhaps the final change to occur while still under the name of Lucas.

Shaftmoor Lane had its fair share of alterations. it began life as a tin shed, the original BW3, and during the course of its life was developed and extended to create BW4. In the 1990s the interior walls were removed and the two factories became one. The personnel and medical block at Shaftmoor Lane, created in 1970, was knocked down in 2003.

Great Hampton Street saw many alterations, in the 1930s in particular. The great flagship lamp factory at Cannock transferred into the hands of an Italian company when Lucas closed, and this has now been turned into a very modern site.

BW4 Shaftmoor Lane, 1935.

Many will remember BW3 and BW4, but people often mistakenly think that they were built at the same time.

Alterations to the Great Hampton Street factory in 1935.

Extension work underway at Great Hampton Street, March 1936.

he medical and personnel block at
haftmoor Lane was built in the 1970s.
is seen here as it was, and in various
ates of demolition.

Great King Street after alterations which too[c] place in the early 1930s.

Below: The view from the Great King Street factory towards Wheeler Street, 1980s.

CHAPTER FOURTEEN
Overseas Connections

Rather than building factories abroad, in many instances Lucas entered into partnerships with foreign companies. Lucas engineers would travel overseas to train and work with established staff, and Lucas's own designs were introduced if in-house products were thought to be inferior. A royalty was paid for Lucas products used under licence. As these were often old designs that had been phased out in the UK, it was useful extra revenue at the end of a product's life.

Despite much success overseas, not all new businesses were successful. In France, for example, attempts to set up a business manufacturing starters were expensive and ended in failure. Much more successful was Lucas's partnership with the German company Bosch, when they used their joint engineering and design resources to produce a new braking system. Germany recalled its engineers just before the Second World War, bringing the partnership to a sudden end. The images below were sent to Oliver and Harry Lucas by Robert Bosch in the late 1930s.

Above: Nazi banners bedeck the flagpoles and swastikas and adorn buildings in Berlin as Hitler's rise to power began, 1930s.

Above, right: Adolf Hitler congratulates Robert Bosch on the ftieth anniversary of the firm at the Berlin Exhibition.

ight: Hitler in conversation with Bosch workmen at the Hotel aiserhof, Berlin.

Above: Delegates from all across the world attended the Lucas Batteries Overseas Operations Convention, held at Chateau Impney Hotel in Droitwich, Worcestershire 1980. Bob Dale is at the centre of the front row. He went on to take over the Lucas Electrical Company as Managing Director.

Bob Dale looks on as the Managing Director of Lucas Brakes (India), Kutty Ramagem, describes the workings of a large truck brake to Secretary of State for Trade and Industry, Peter Lilley, early 1990s.

he Rossi factory, São Paolo, razil, 1981. Rossi was n ailing concern before it ined forces with Lucas, nanufacturing lighting quipment. Lionel Rossi emained as financial director, nd Lucas provided the other xecutives. Tom Gannon was ie local director, in charge f all engineering aspects, while David Barrow was chief xecutive. He remained in ritain, and only visited Brazil nce a year.

Lucas engineers at the Martin Amarto factory, Argentina. Seen here are Bob Lilley, Peter Bates, the Manager of the Amarto factory, Dave Boot and two other unknown engineers.

he Detroit branch, 1982. icas New King Street situated outside the ain city of Detroit in a wn called, appropriately ough, Birmingham.

LUCAS Service in Australia
Messrs Bennett & Wood Ltd.,   Our Sydney Service Agents

(1) Service Garage; (2) Exterior of Service Station, Wentworth Avenue, Sydney; (3) General Electrical Repair Shop; (4) Sales Dept; (5) Battery Repair Dept. and (6) Charging Room.

Advertising material showing services offered by some of Lucas's furthest outposts in Sydney and Melbourne, 1930s. Lucas's international presence also included factories in Canada, France, Germany, China, Japan and Russia.

LUCAS Service in Australia
LUCAS Sales & Service Pty. Ltd, Melbourne, Victoria.

The Exterior of the Service Station

The General Stores

Some of the members of the Staff outside their offices

A photograph of part of the Service Garage

USE AND STOCK ONLY GENUINE LUCAS SPARES